GYOTABSTRACT INTRODUCTION

Gyotabstract? What does that mean?!? It is a term I created. It is a combination of Gyotaku and abstract. Gyotaku is Japanese fish printing. Before the advent of the camera Japanese fisherman used this century old printmaking technique to document their catch while they were still on the boat.

After they catch the fish , it is then inked with either ink or acrylic paint using a brayer or a brush. A brayer is like a small rolling pin used to spread the ink on the fish. See figure 1 for what these tools look like. A brush could also be used to ink the fish. After you have an even coat of ink or paint on the fish the fisherman used either the spoon or baren to press the paper on the fish, see figure 2. A baren is a round disc that has a handle to firmly press the paper on the fish. Usually really thin paper was used, rice paper was traditionally used. After you pressed the paper on the fish and peeled it away you got an impression from it. Congratulations you created a Gyotaku print.

That is a brief exclamation of how to create a Gyotaku print but that is just the first half of my term GYOTABSTRACT the other half being ABSTRACT. ABSTRACT stands for abstract painting. Around and on the fish print I have used either the brayer or the brush to paint "abstractly" on the fish print.

THAT IS ABOUT IT FOR EXPLAINING THE TECHNIQUE OF GYOTABSTRACT. THIS IS NOT A HOW TO BOOK BUT RATHER IT IS A CHANCE TO SHOWCASE THIS UNIQUE ARTWORK ALL IN ONE PLACE. A MOBILE GALLERY OF MY GYOTABSTRACT !!! I HOPE YOU ENJOY IT !! THANKS FOR LOOKING, PATRICK B. HUMPHREYS.

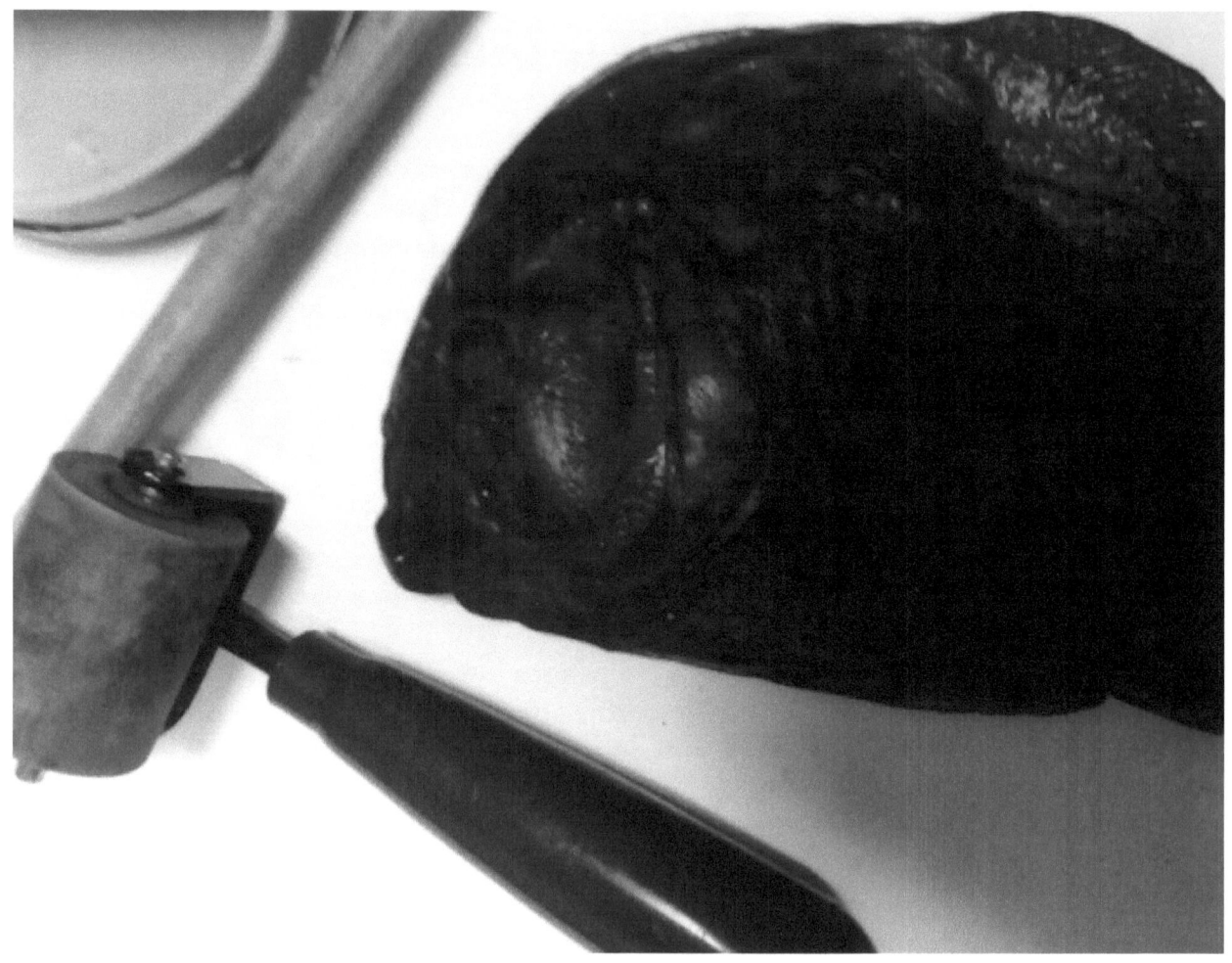

Figure 1- this photograph shows a fish mold (this mold is of a piranha), and a brayer. The brayer looks like a small rolling pin.

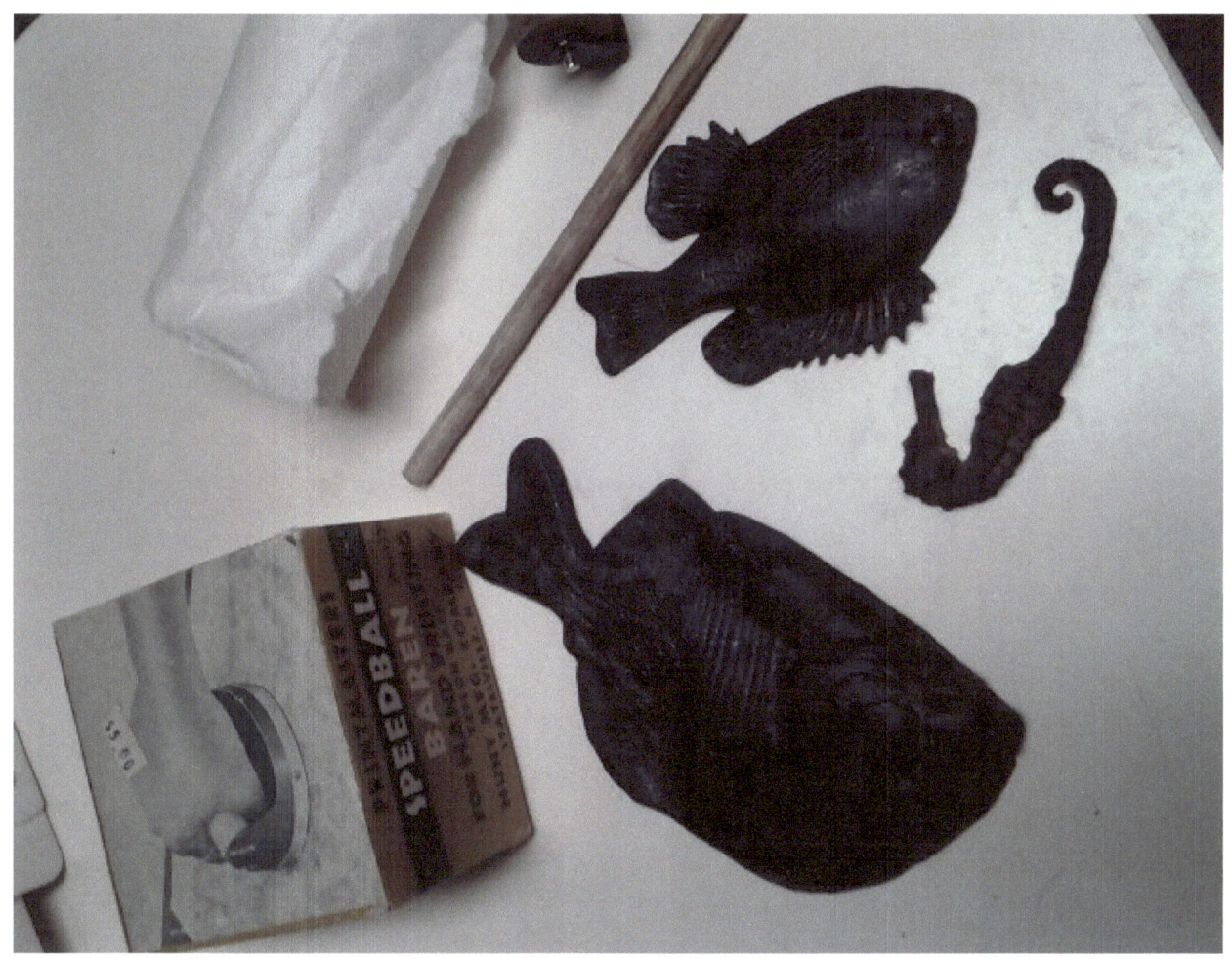

Figure 2- this photograph shows the same piranha fish mold as well as a seahorse and small trout. These fish molds were purchased online at *www.dickblick.com*. Also in the picture is the baren (inside a box) , a wooden spoon and a roll of rice paper to print the fish on.

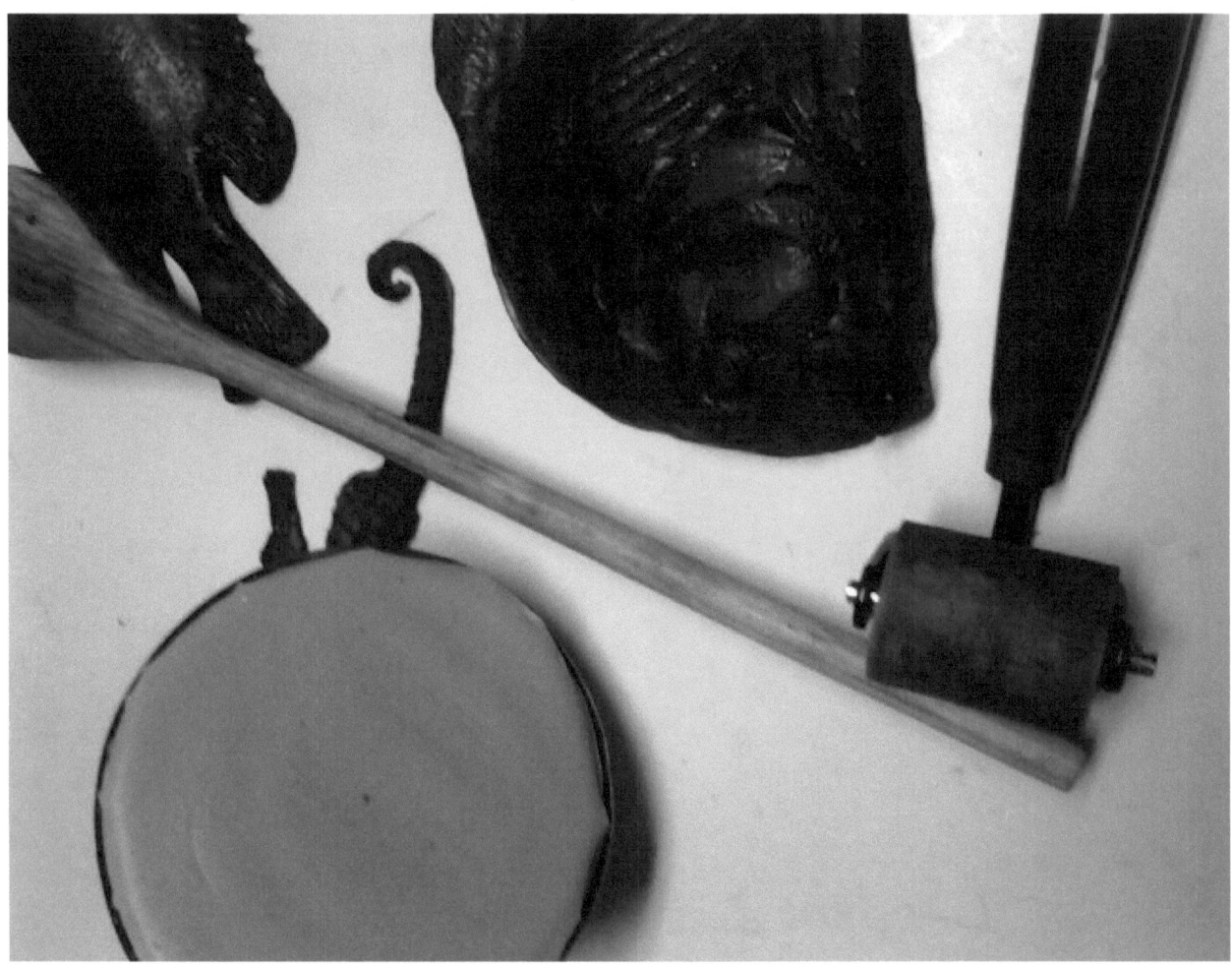

Figure 3- in this photograph the baren is out of the box. Notice the small circular bottom that is used to create pressure on the paper to get a good impression from the fish.

THE PLATES

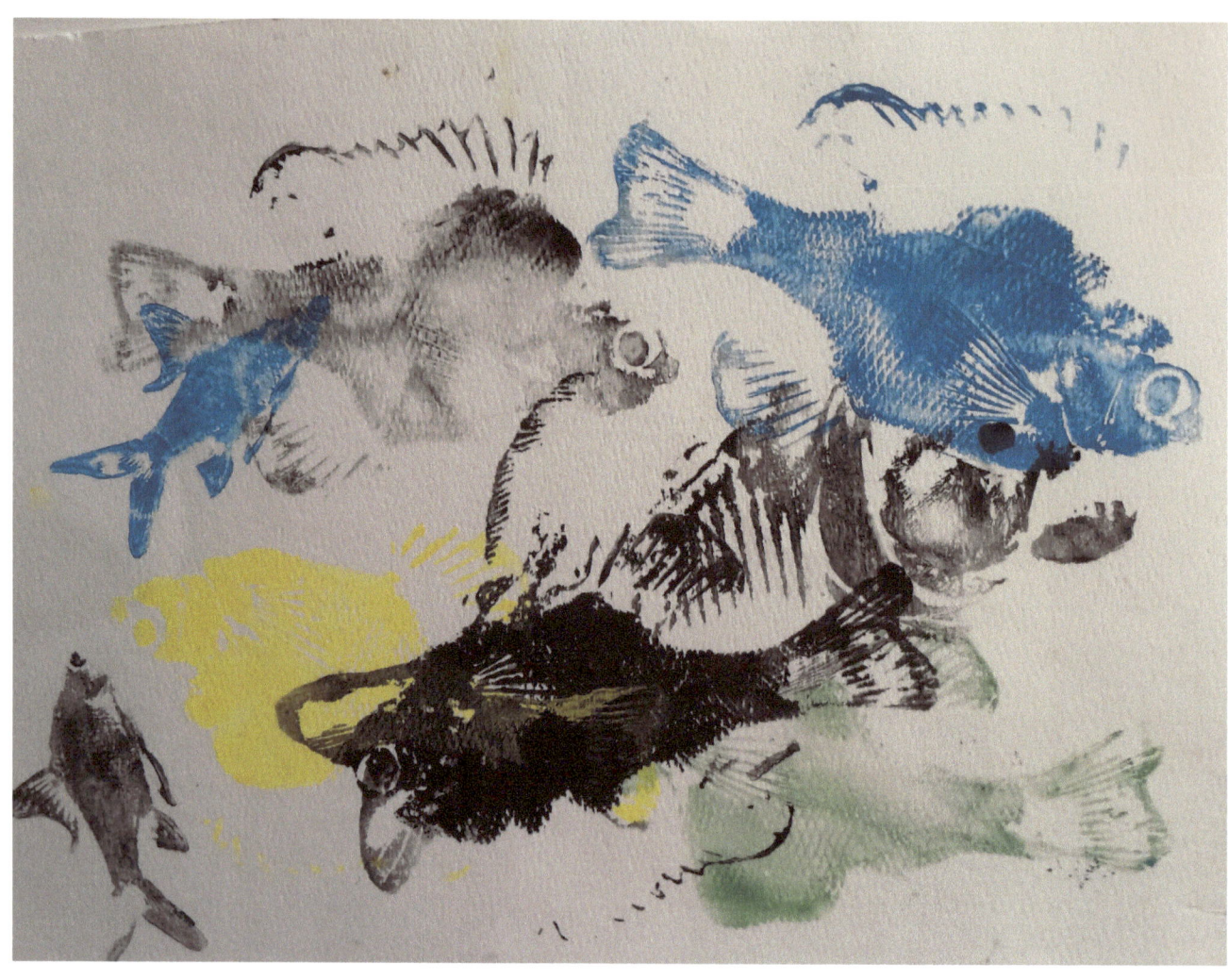

Figure 4- this image is an early one of GYOTABSTRACT. Notice how I printed the whole fish and lots of them !! A school of them !! I left a lot of negative space or white space. This image as well as the other images in this book were printed on thick watercolor paper. I find the watercolor paper hold up better with the painting technique in the following images.

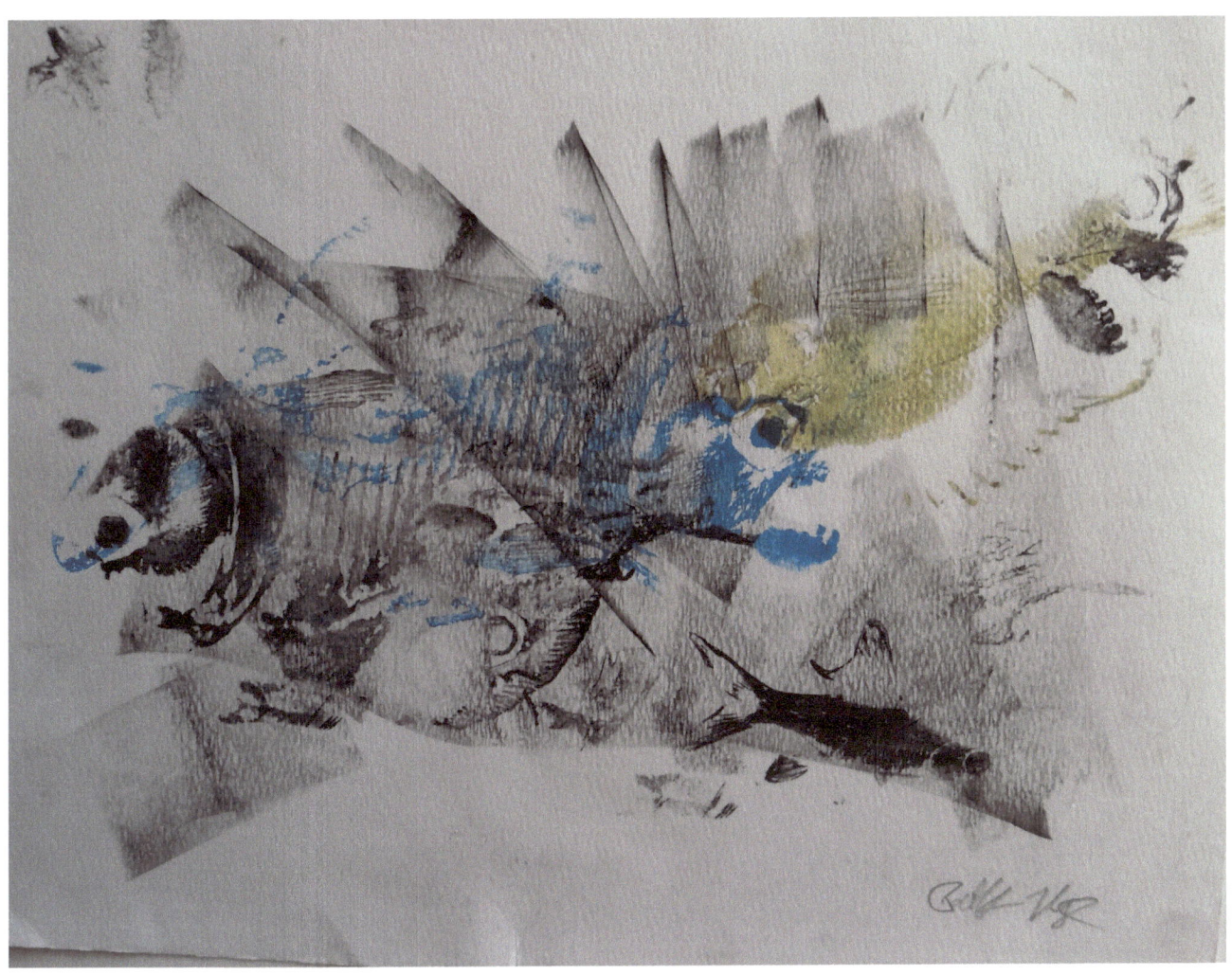

Figure 5- this image has not only the fish printing but it has the abstract painting on it. I used the side of the brayer as a painting instrument. This image I also signed my name in the lower right hand corner. The way a traditional print is signed but in reality this is a MONOPRINT : a SINGLE PRINT. A one of a kind piece of GYOTABSTRACT.

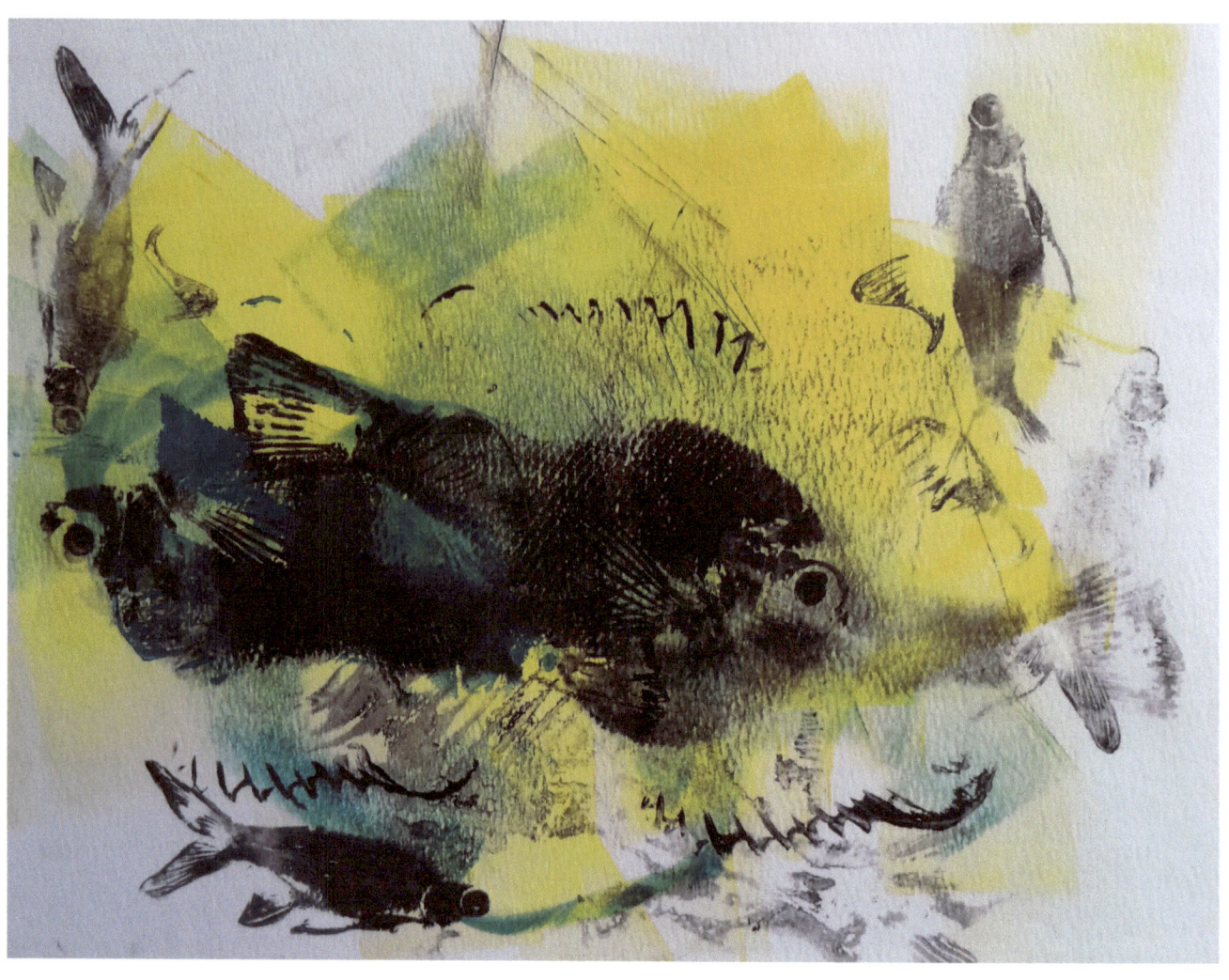

Figure 6 – this image is even more abstract then the previous one. There is not much negative space in fact yellow covers most of the background.

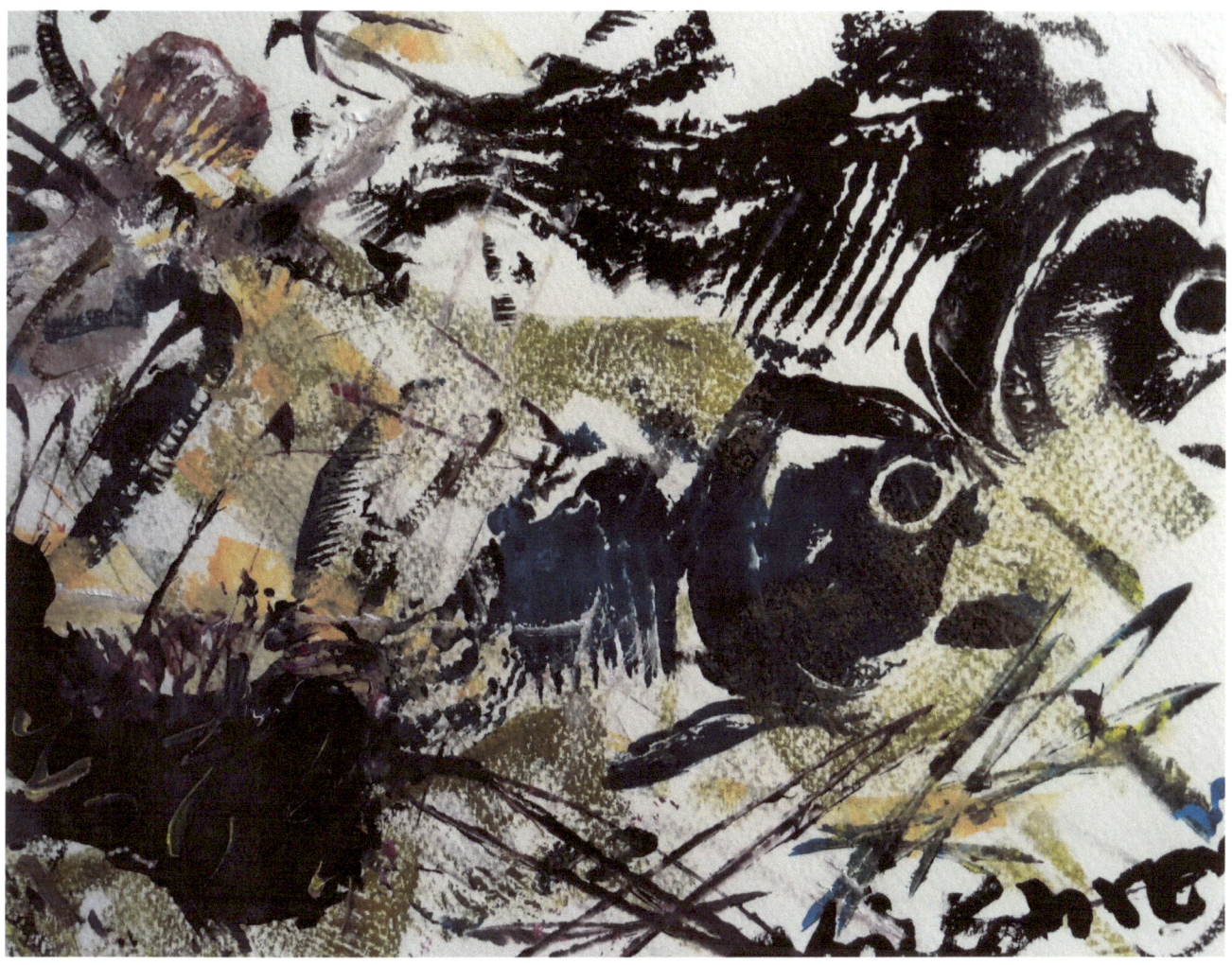

Figure 7 – this image is much more abstract then the previous ones. The fish is almost "lost in a sea of abstraction". This is from a sketchbook of mine. The image is rather small : 8"x6" but in this context it seems monumental.

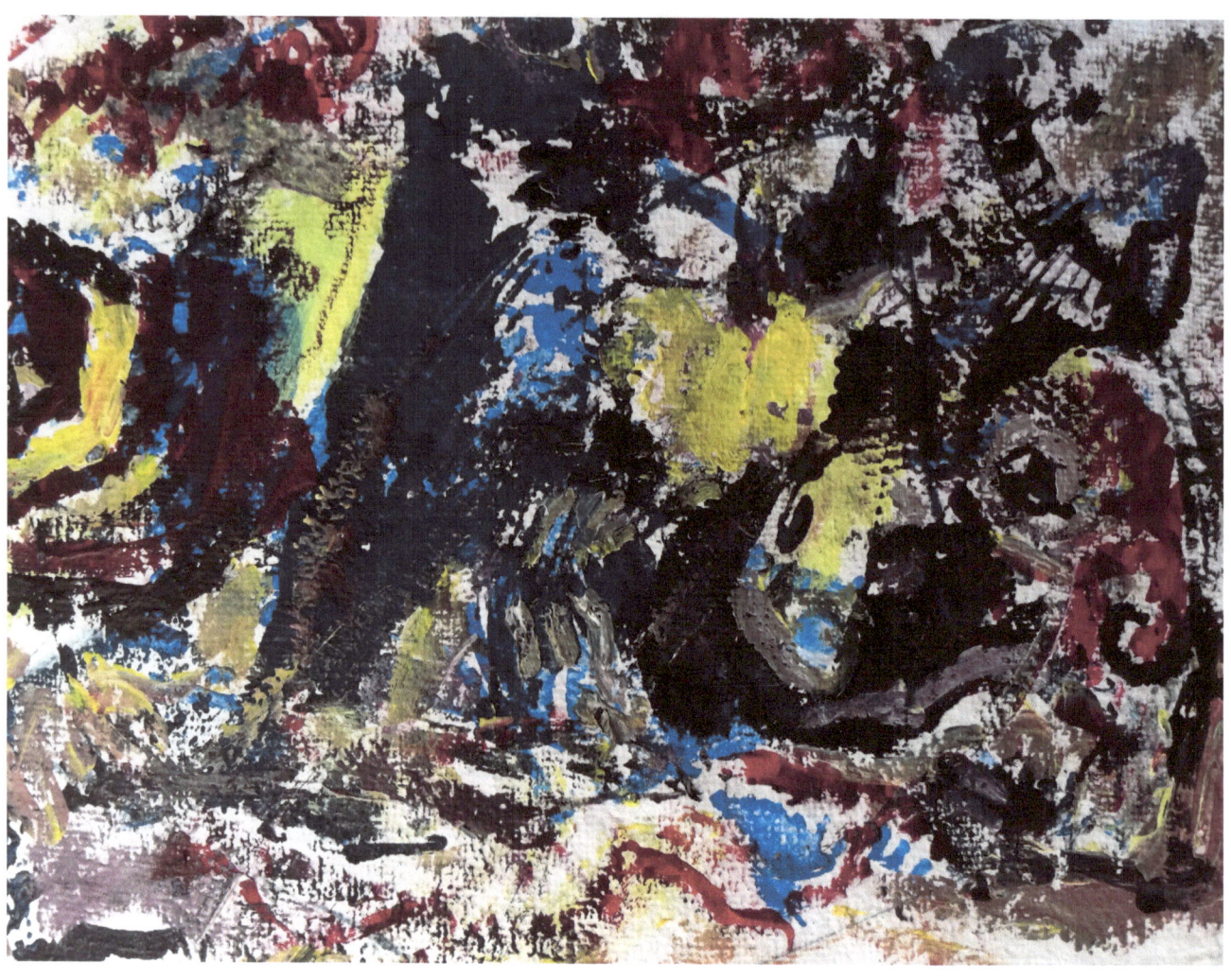

FIGURE 8 – *this image again is very "abstract". The fish is all but "lost". The abstract painting took over the painting. The fish are hardly recognizable at all. It is hardly a print at all but is almost just an abstract painting not that is a bad thing just bad in the context of this book.*

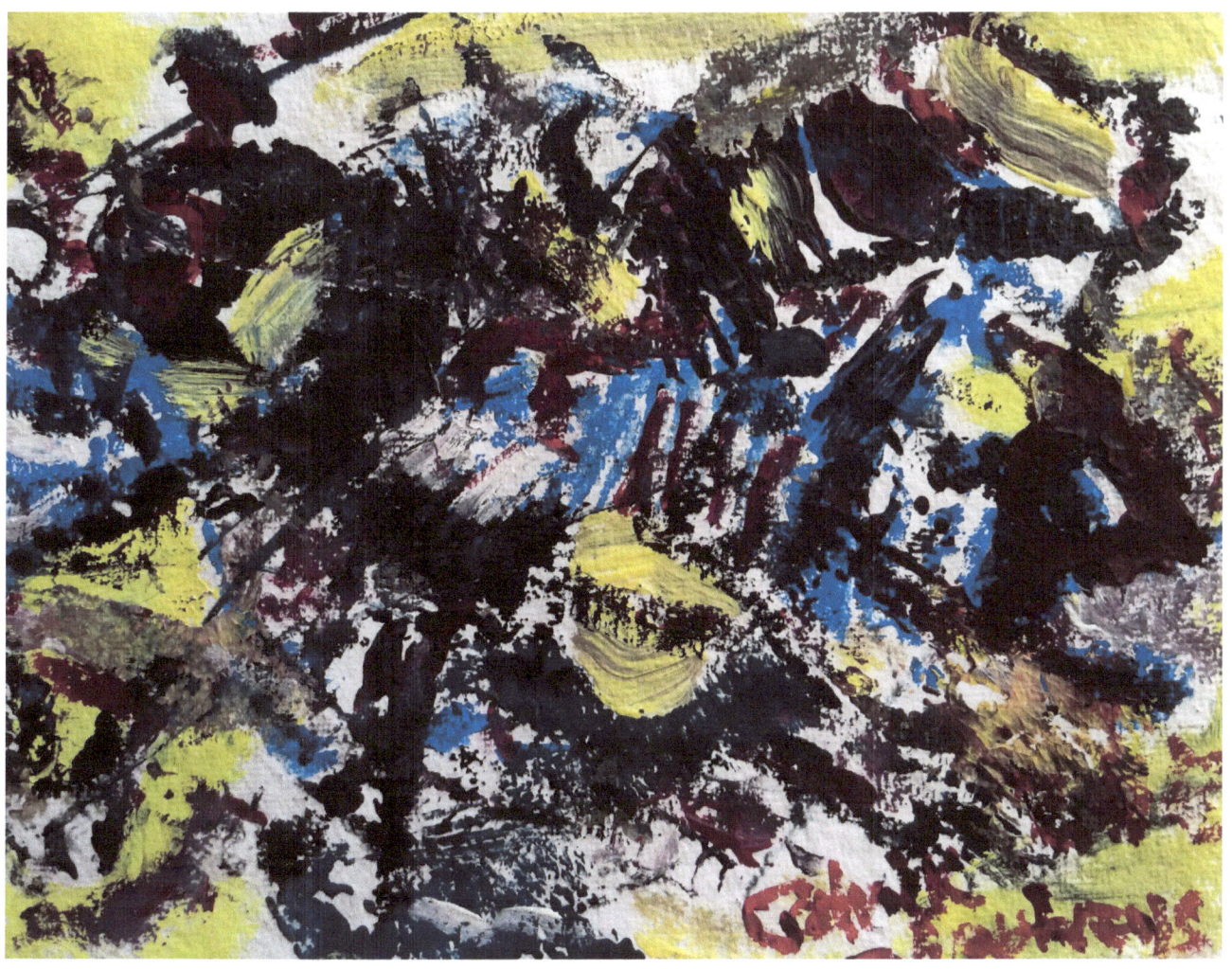

Figure 9 – this image the fish is more "recognizable" . The black fish head on the right side with its body evident in the other side of the image. The background is more "organized" . The color yellow is dominate in the background . The yellow unifies the image together. It gives "flesh" to the fish.

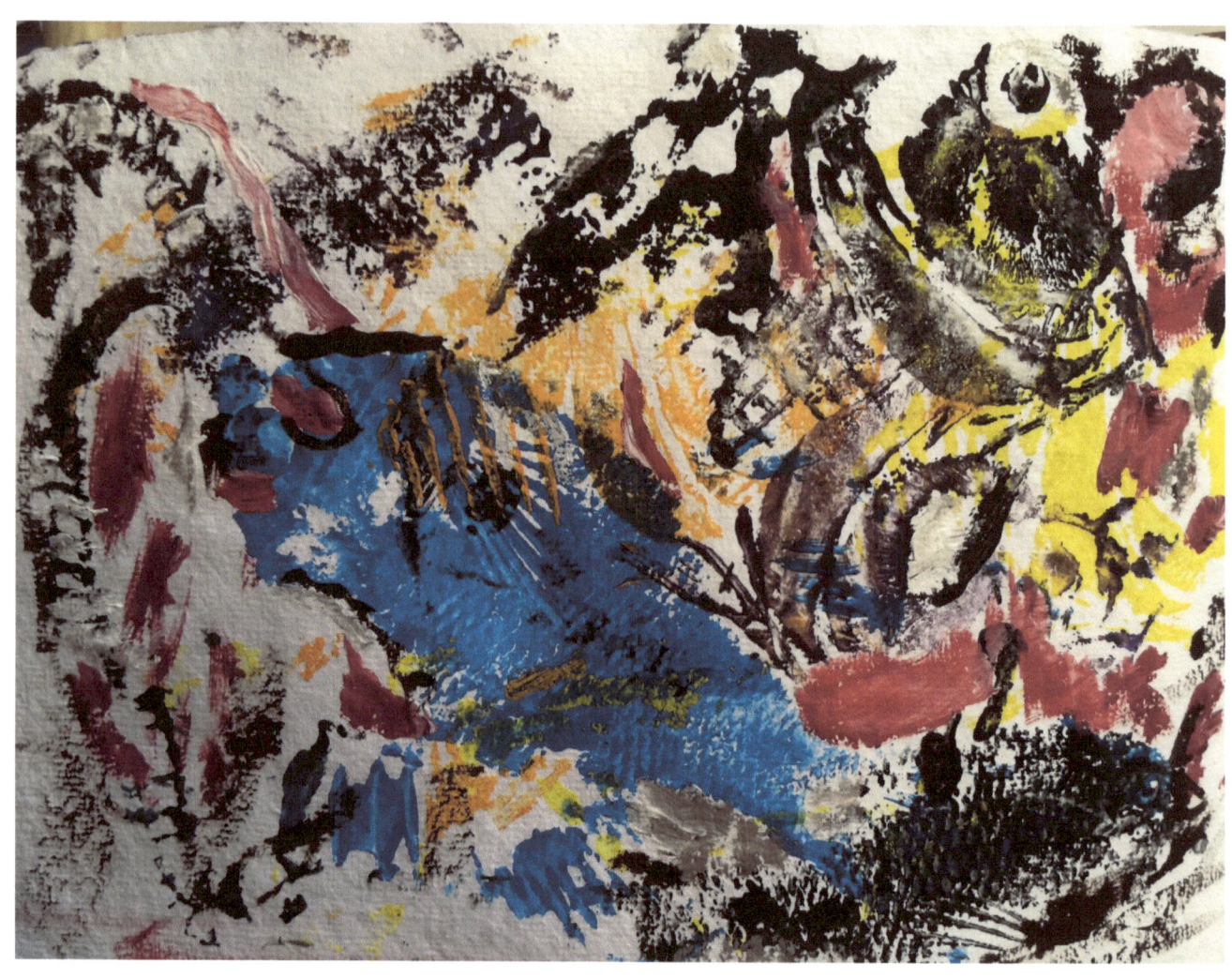

Figure 10- this image the fish is "caught" !! That is the fish is more evident in the image. It is not "lost in a sea of abstraction". I "caught" your attention with this image !!! (At least I hope I did) !!!

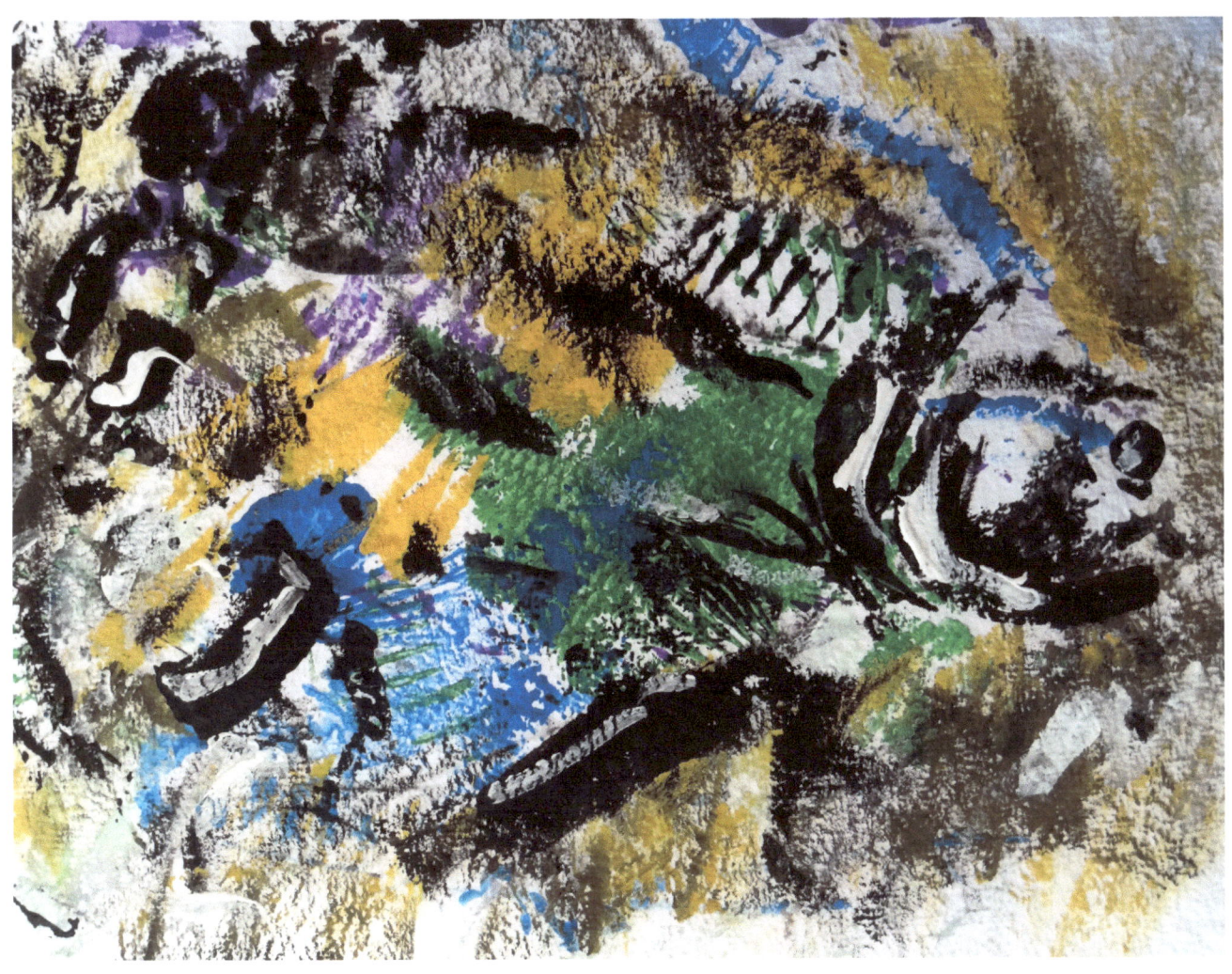

Figure 11- the fish is more easily "caught" in this picture. The background is more organized making the fish "pop out" from the background. This image also includes another element that wasn't in the previous ones : LETTERS. I used a stencil to create the letters. Only one letter is recognizable : a **G** . There are other pieces of letters but the "G" is the only letter that can be "read".

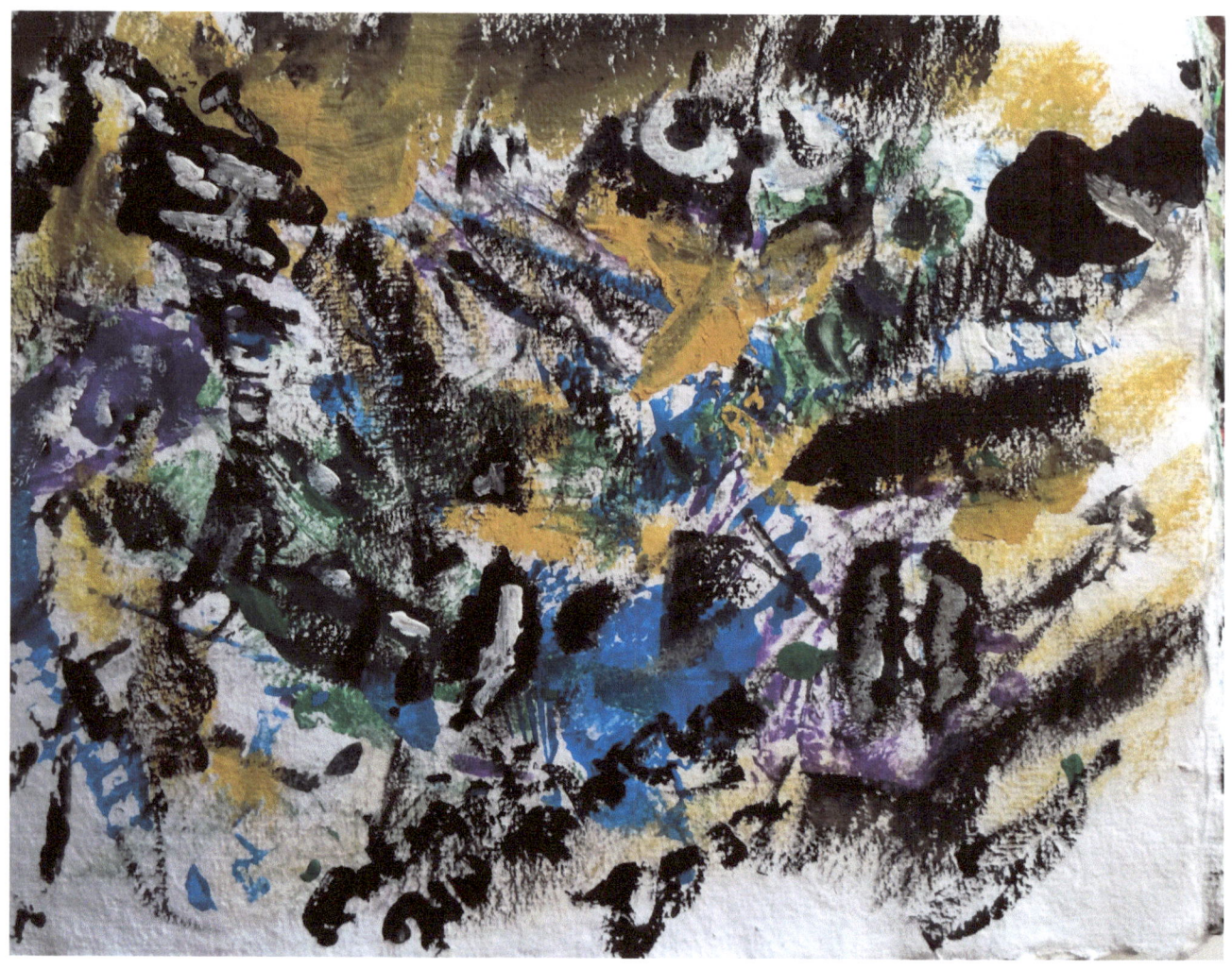

Figure 12- this image you can read the letters : G , B and H but the fish is "lost in a sea of abstraction". My signature is evident in this image in fact it is rather large part of the image akin to the signature Vincent in the image of "Sunflowers in a vase" by Vincent Van Gogh (one of the artists I greatly admire).

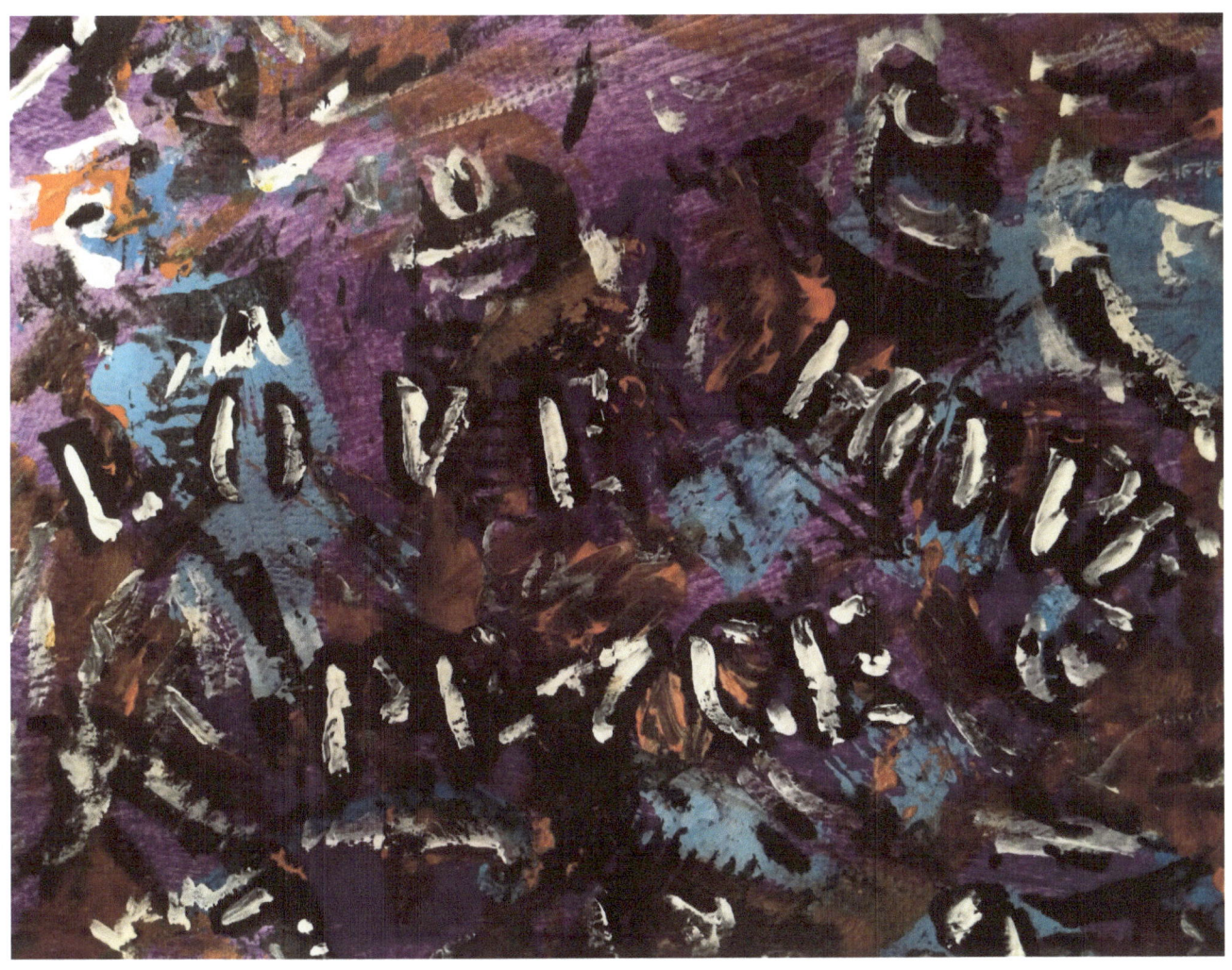

Figure 13- this image is very different from the previous ones in several ways. Firstly you can read the words in this image IT SAYS LOVE HATE PEACE. Also the background is a solid color (purple). It unifies the image but I don't think it "works" very well. The purple isn't the right color but I LOVE HATE PEACE IT !!!!

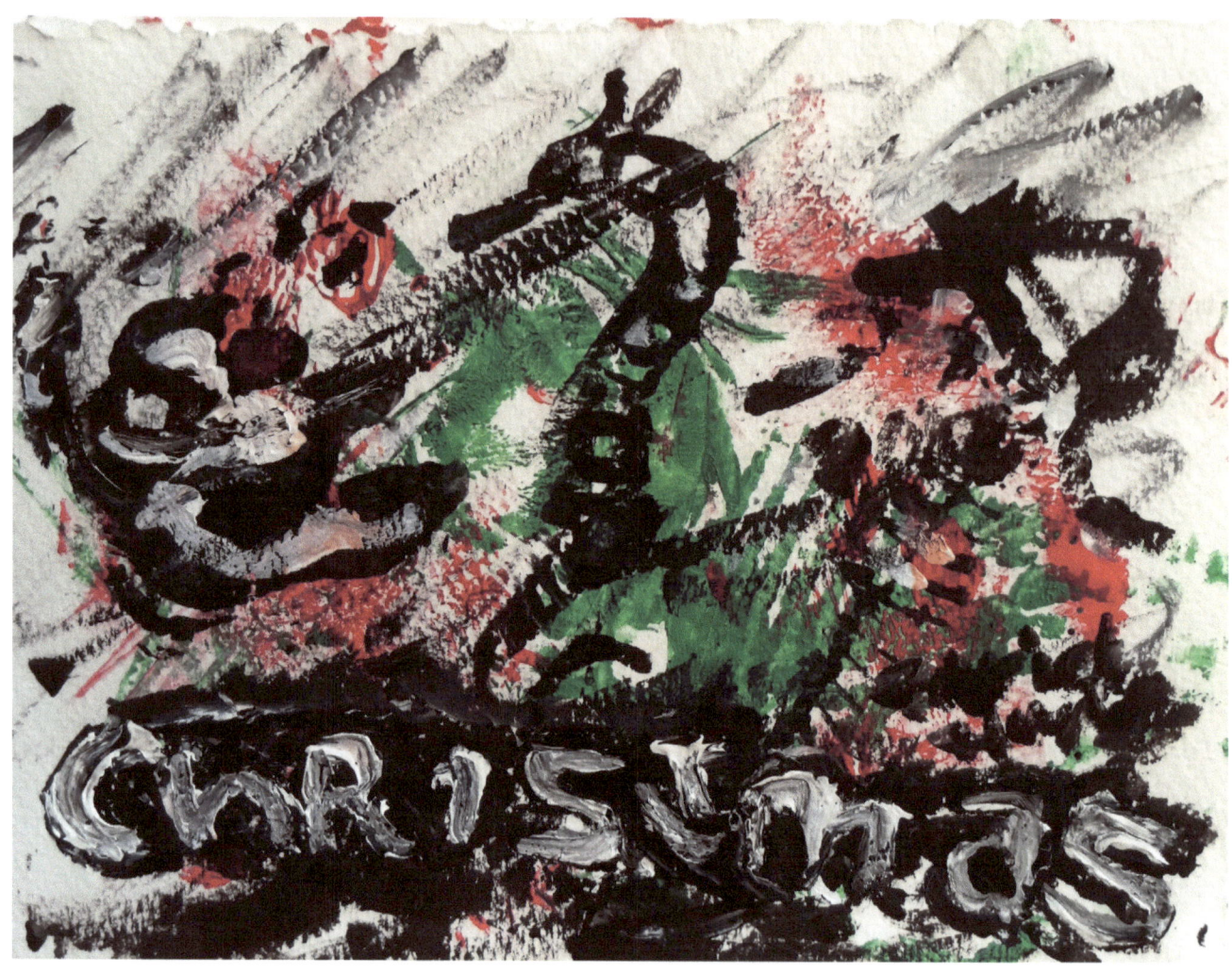

Figure 14- this image was created as a response from a friend to do a Christmas image. This is what I created. A seahorse is the central image with the main colors used are green and red . Colors you relate to Christmas. Red the color of Santa Claus and green the color of the Christmas tree. The seahorse is my take on the subject. Perhaps Santa is supposed to ride a seahorse and not reindeer ??? Well, maybe ????

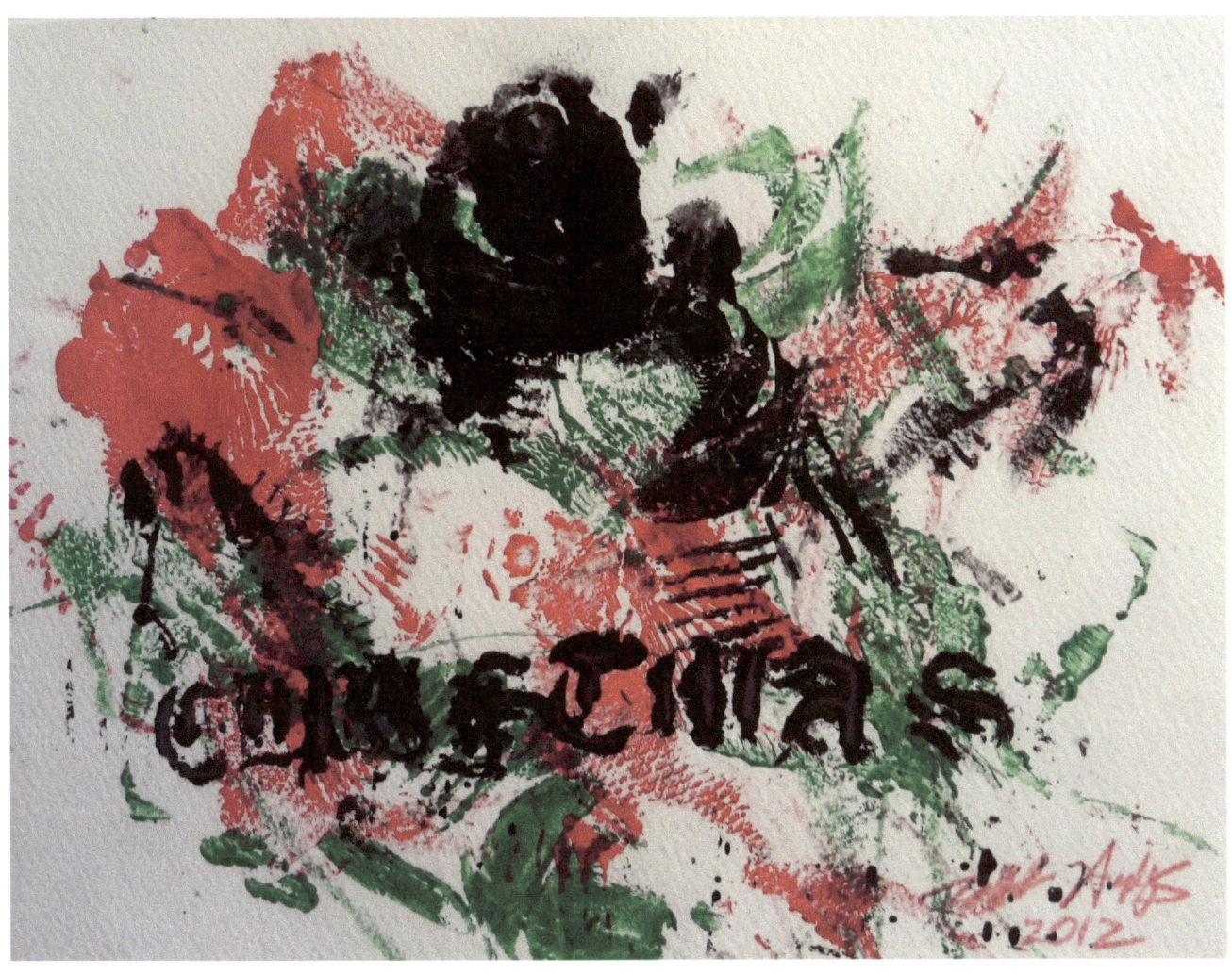

Figure 15 – another image inspired by Christmas . Just like the other one, the central figure is a fish but this time the fish is a piranha and not a seahorse. Santa the piranha ?!? Maybe ?!? Maybe not ?!? Only thing I know for sure is that I don't want to be on his NAUGHTY LIST ! SO YOU BETTER BE GOOD FOR GOODNESS SAKE !!!!!

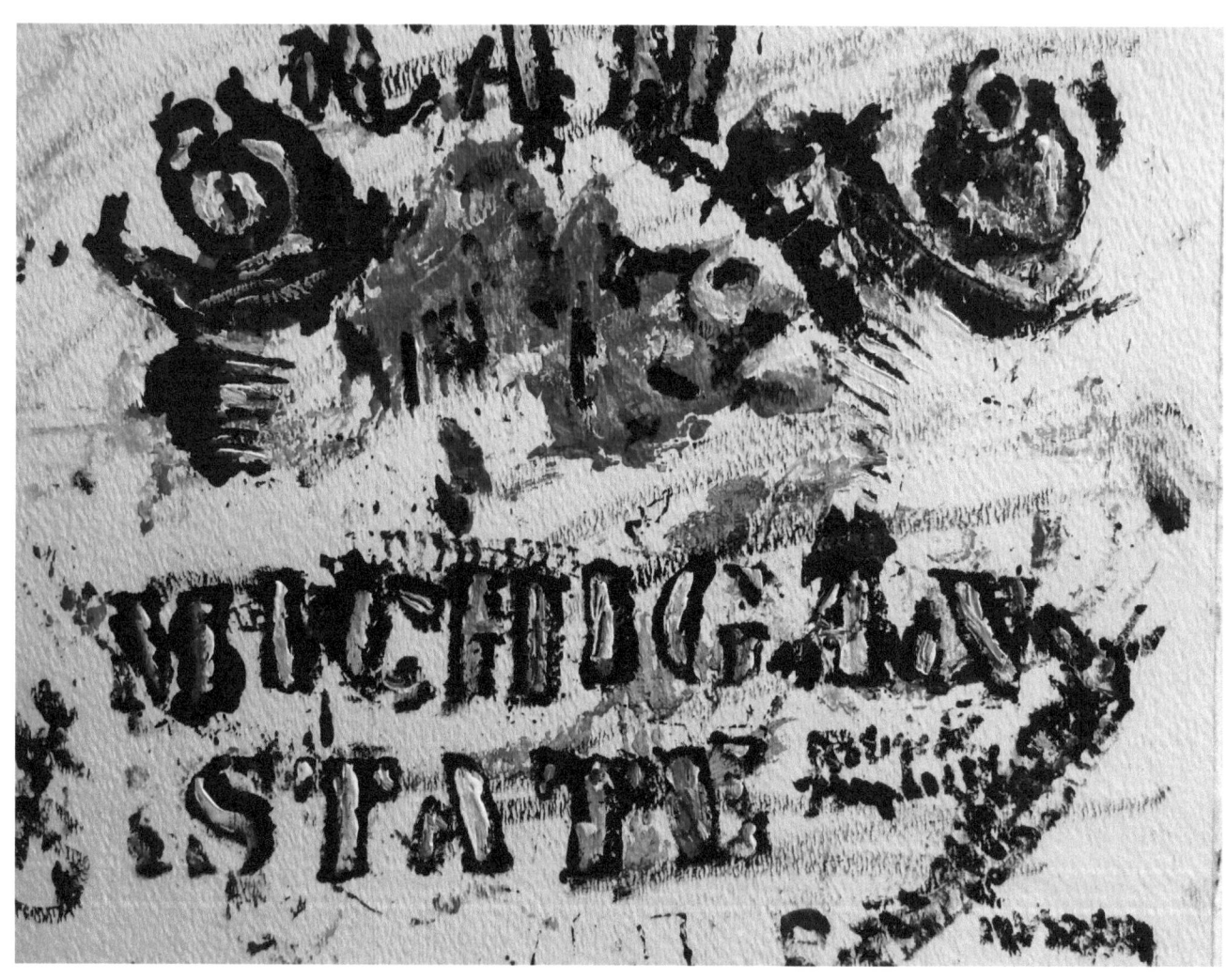

Figure 16- this image is inspired by my son, Cameron who at the time of writing this book is 11 years old. Currently we live in Bay City, Michigan and Cameron loves Michigan State University. He said he would like to go there when he gets older but the main reason he likes them is for their sports teams in particular the football team. This image is the response to that sentiment. There are two main piranhas in the image with the words Michigan State at the bottom and Cam at the top. GO SPARTANS !! GO GREEN AND WHITE !!!!!

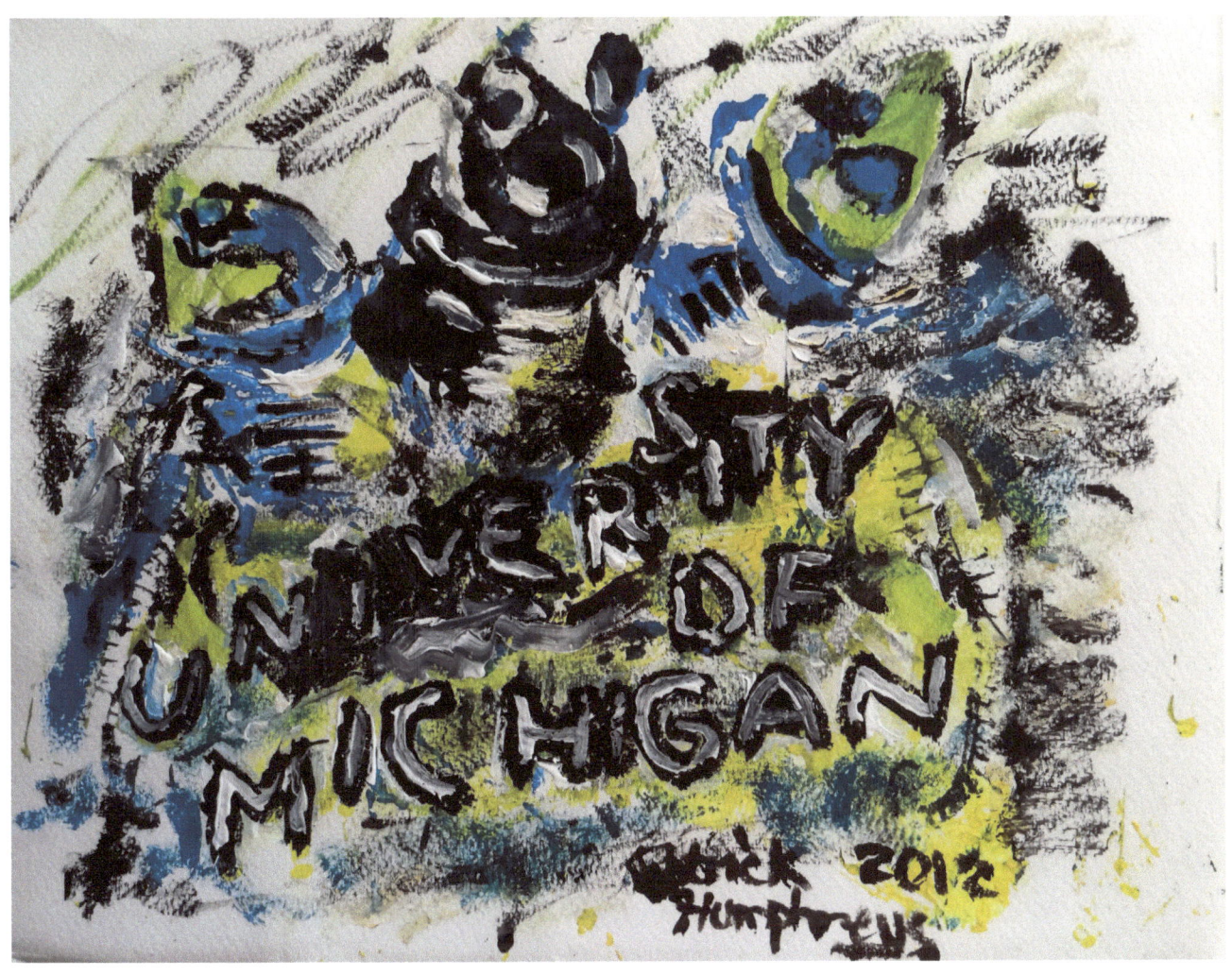

Figure 17- this image was made as a response to the other university in Michigan : the University of Michigan. THERE ARE NO WOLVERINES HERE !! But rather there are three fish in the top (piranhas to be exact) with the words UNIVERSITY OF MICHIGAN AND MY SIGNATURE PAINTED WITH PAINT INSTEAD OF SIGNED WITH PENCIL. GO WOLVERINES !!!! GO BLUE AND GOLD !!! (ENOUGH OF THAT !!!) !!!!

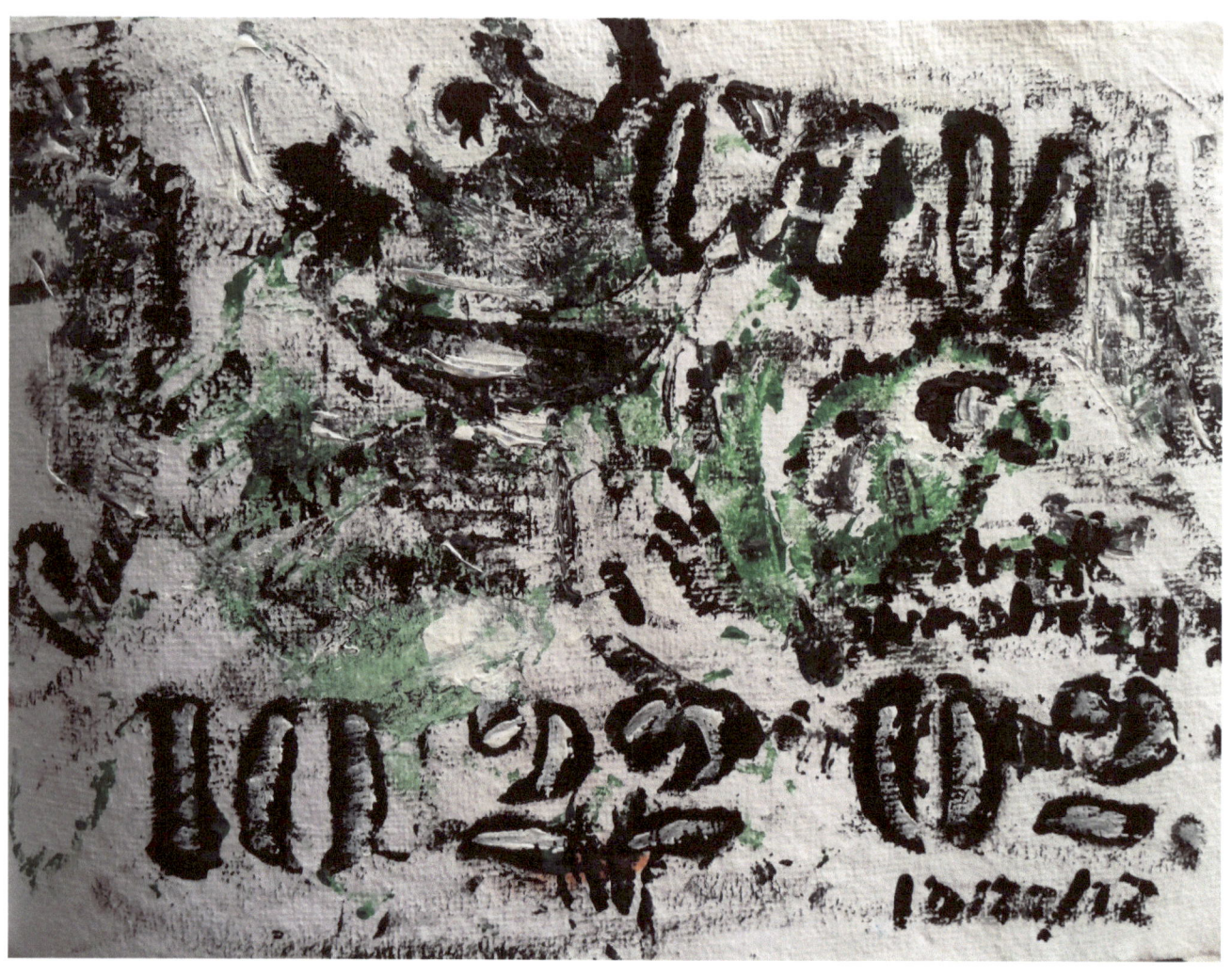

Figure 18- this image is a response to my son, Cameron and his love of Michigan State University. There are the words CAM and the numbers 10, 22, 02. The significance of these numbers is that these numbers are the birthday of Cameron. The words and not the fish image are the main focus of the image. THIS IMAGE IS MEANT TO BE READ !! GO GREEN AND WHITE !! GO CAM !!!!

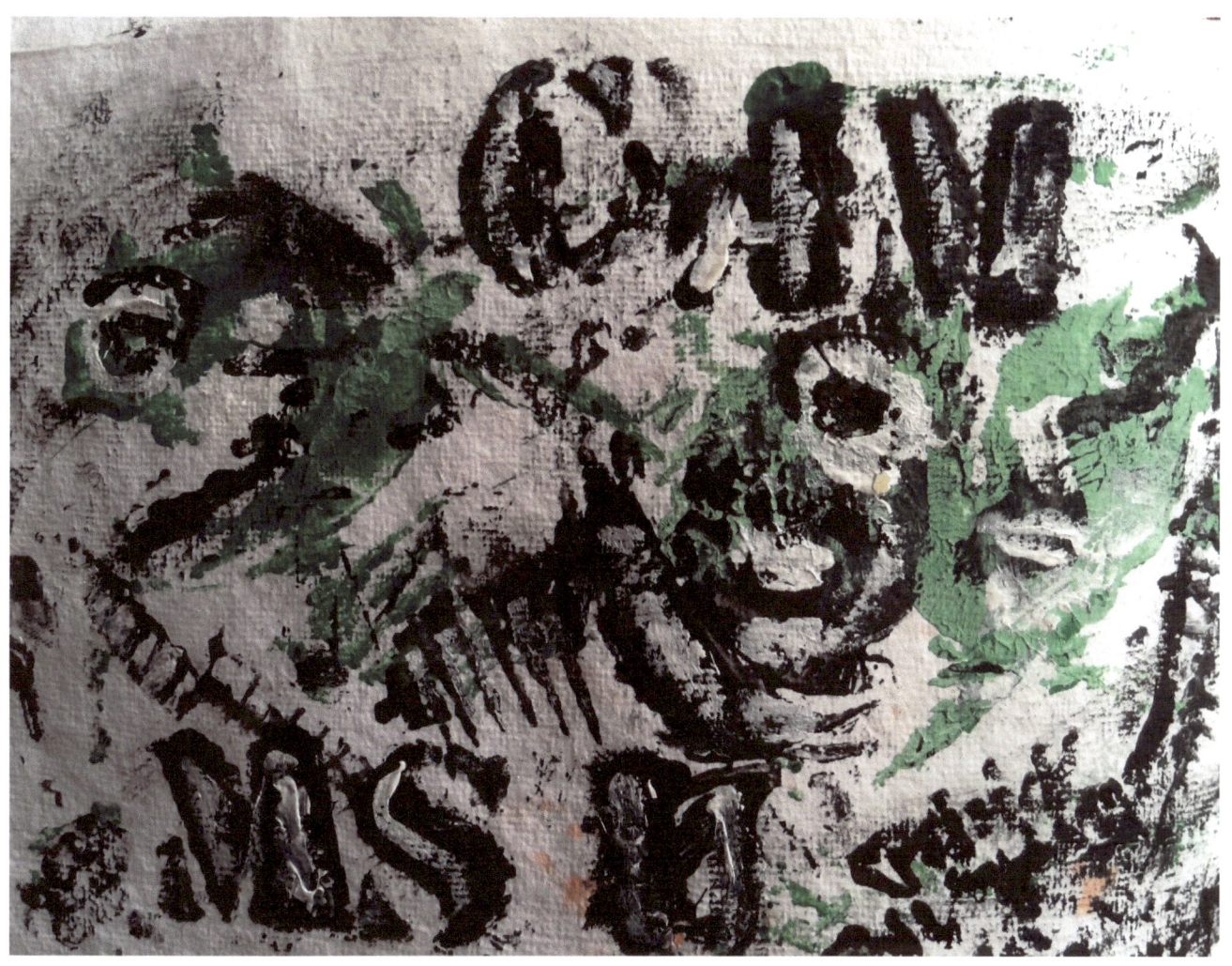

Figure 19- this is another image I created for my son, Cameron. This image has the letter MSU and CAM on the top with a faint impression of a piranha like figure 18 this image was meant to be read. GO MSU !!! GO CAM !!! YEA !!! YEA!!! (PUT LYRICS FOR FIGHT SONG HERE ??!!???). MAYBE NOT !?!!???

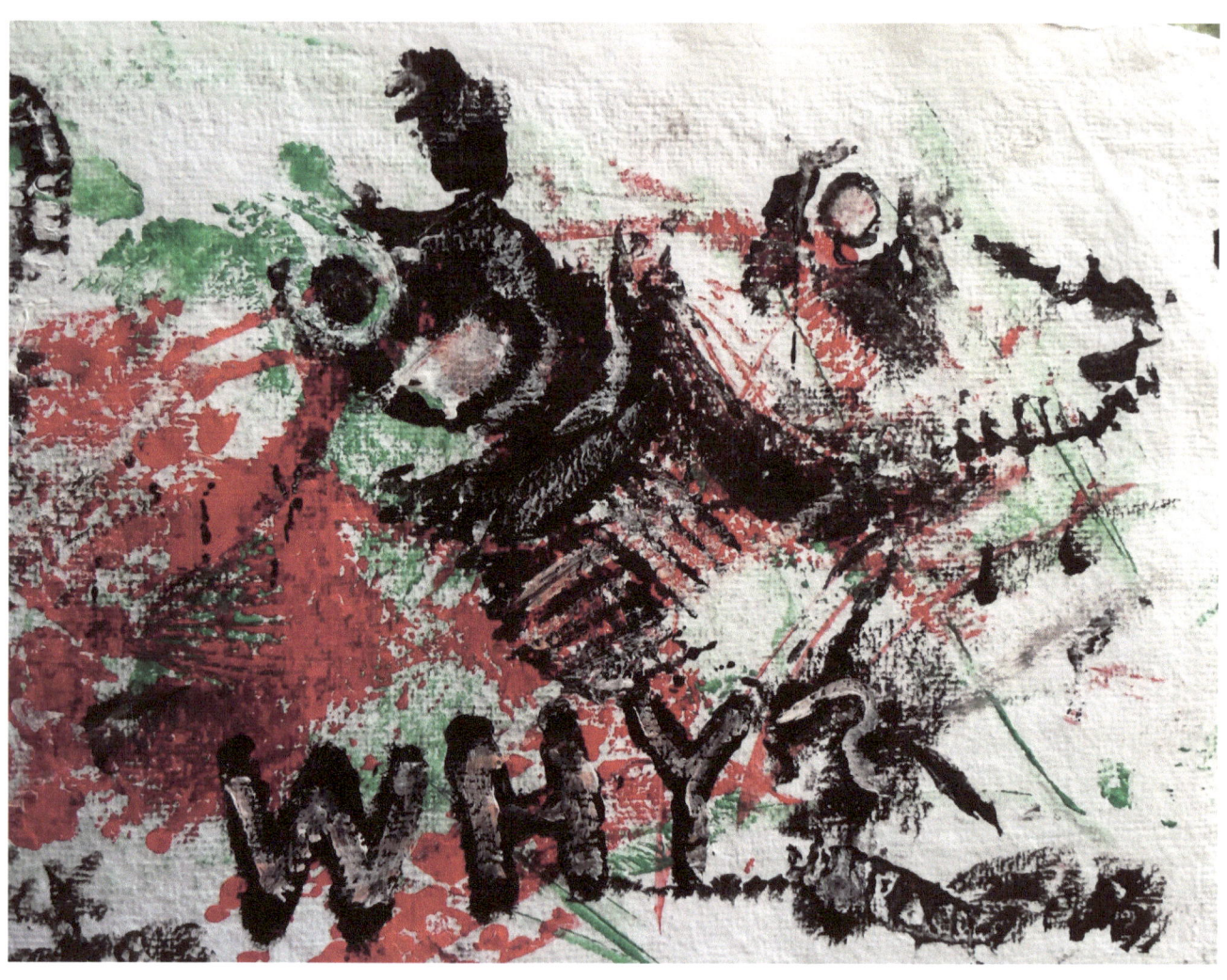

Figure 20 – well that's about enough of the colleges !!! What is this image ?!? NOT WHAT BUT WHY ??!!? IT IS WRITTEN WHY ? But why , YOU DECIDE ?!? There are two distinct fish in this image. Piranhas in fact. I think you can guess by now what is my favorite fish to print is ? This image the background is more integrated with the piranha and the words . It "works" as a complete image . BUT WHY ?

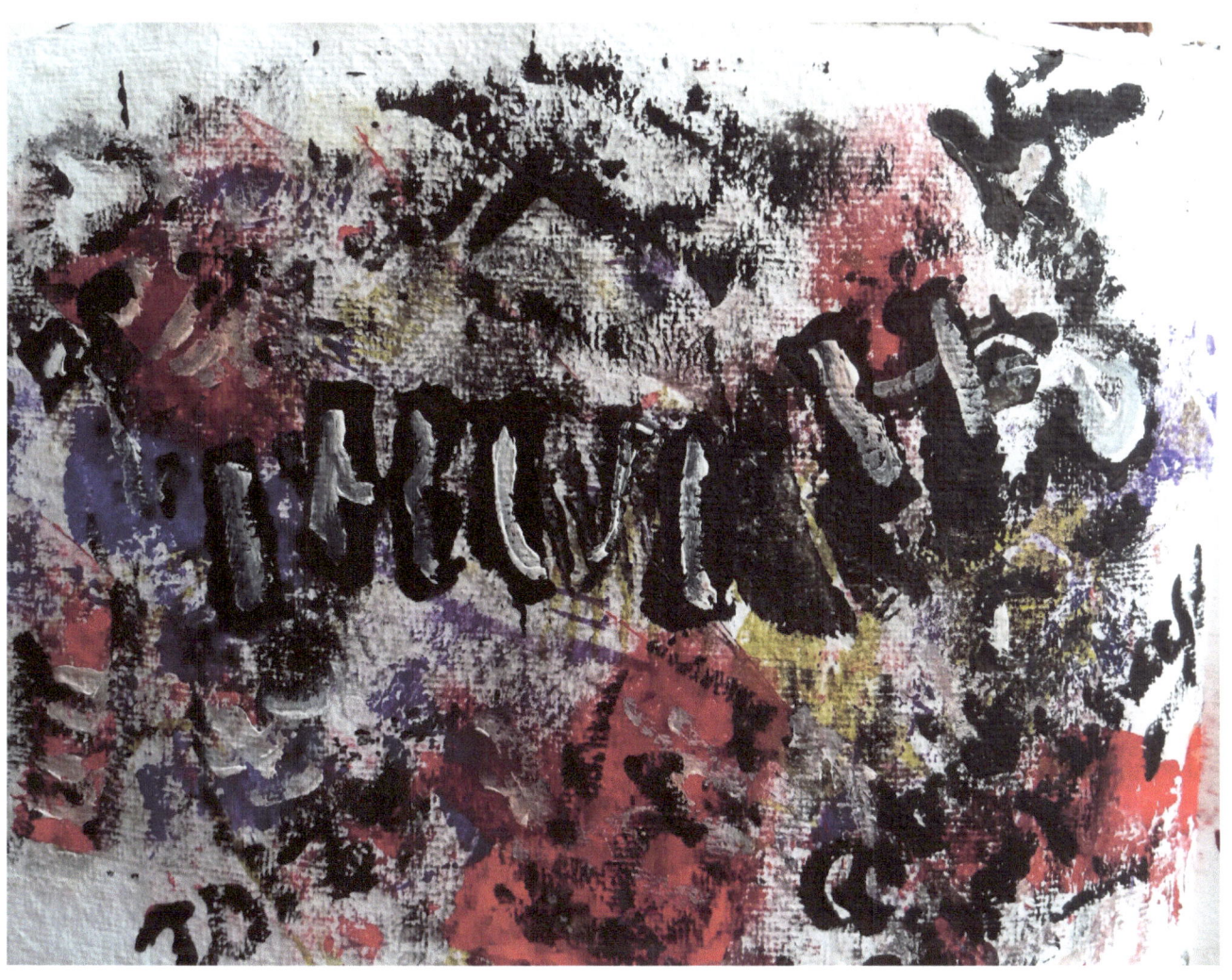

Figure 21- just like figure 20 this image asks a question HUH ? Is huh really a word ?
Yes the definition is "an exclamation of derision , bewilderment, inquiry, etc... It
makes you wonder looking at it HUH ?!? Just like the previous image this one is meant
to READ. The image of the fish is not that evident . I LEAVE IT UP TO THE VIEWER TO
DECIDE ITS MEANING !!!

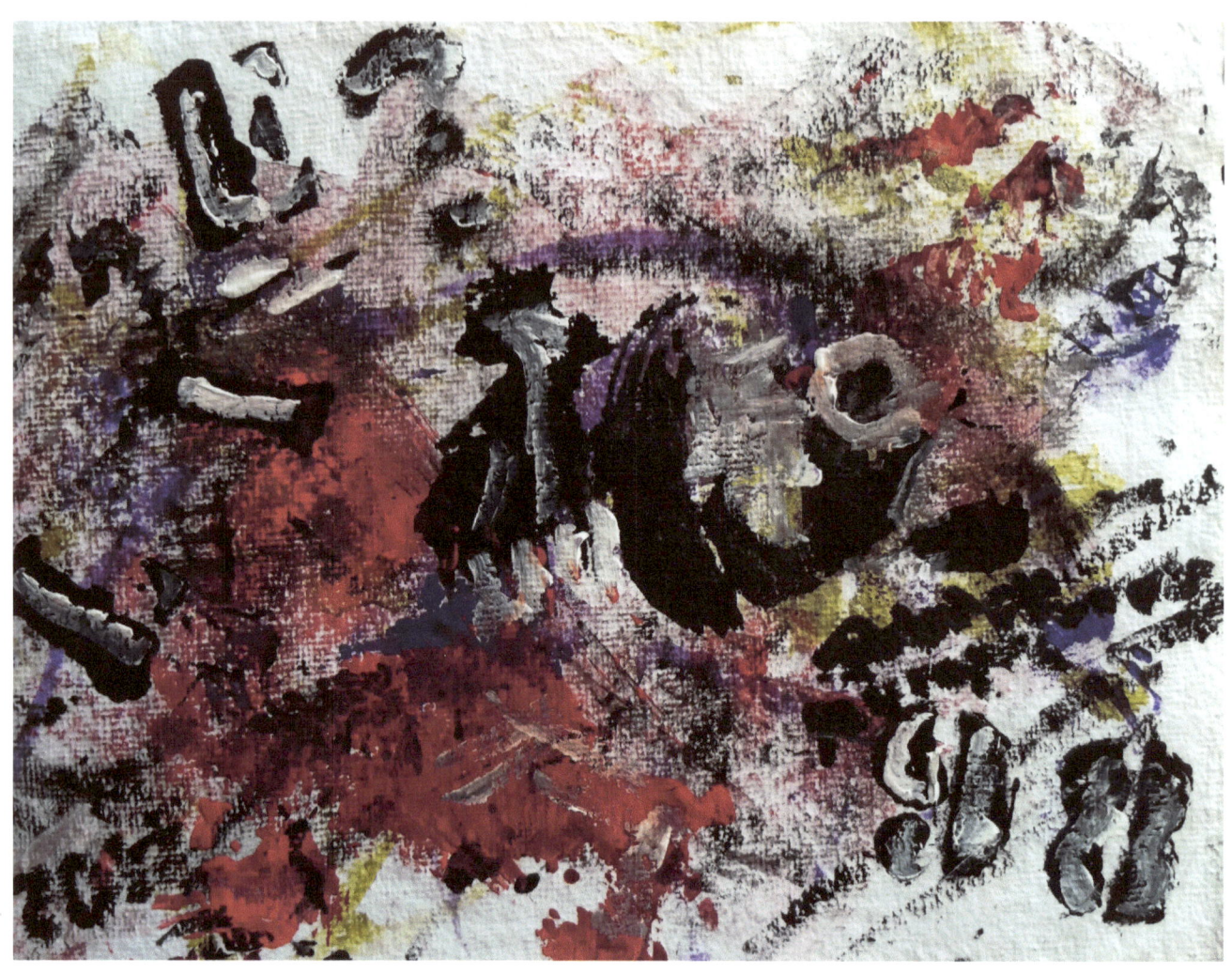

Figure 22- this image the most dominate thing is the piranha and the numbers 98 . The significance of this number is the year I got married and the year of my divorce was 2012. The year I created this image. Another book I got published " Divorce Diary " by CreateSpace Publishing, ISBN : 978-1484030257, 2013. This image was inspired by my divorce. THE COLOR RED IS DOMINATE SIGNIFY MY HEART BEING RIPPED OUT . THE FISH BEING A PIRANHA BEING MY EX WIFE BEING VICIOUS !!! DO I SOUND BITTER ?! NO !!!???!!!!

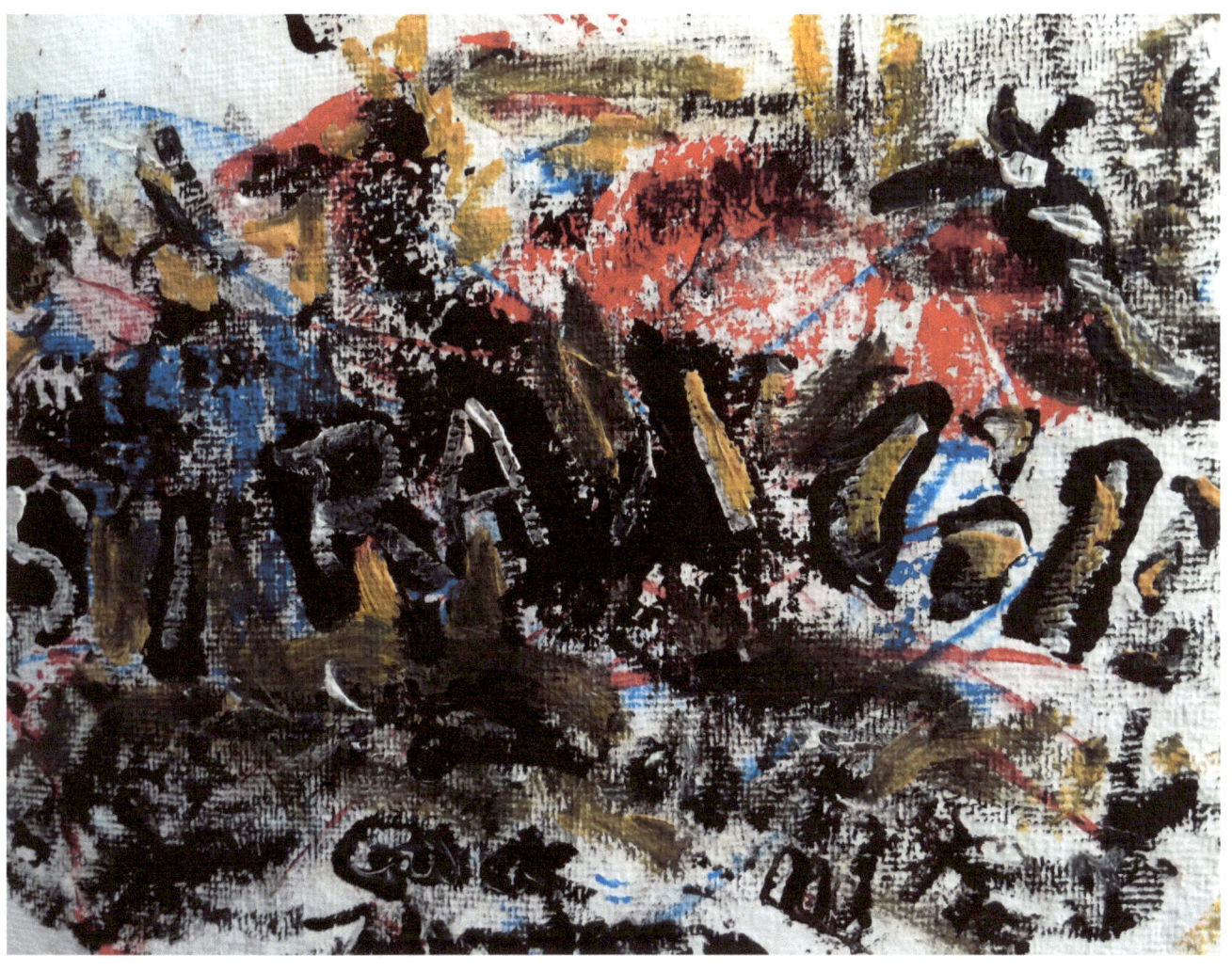

Figure 24- this image is STRANGE. That is the word "STRANGE" is the dominate element in the image. You can see a couple of black seahorses in the background but the first thing you see is STRANGE. You decide if it is STRANGE or NOT.

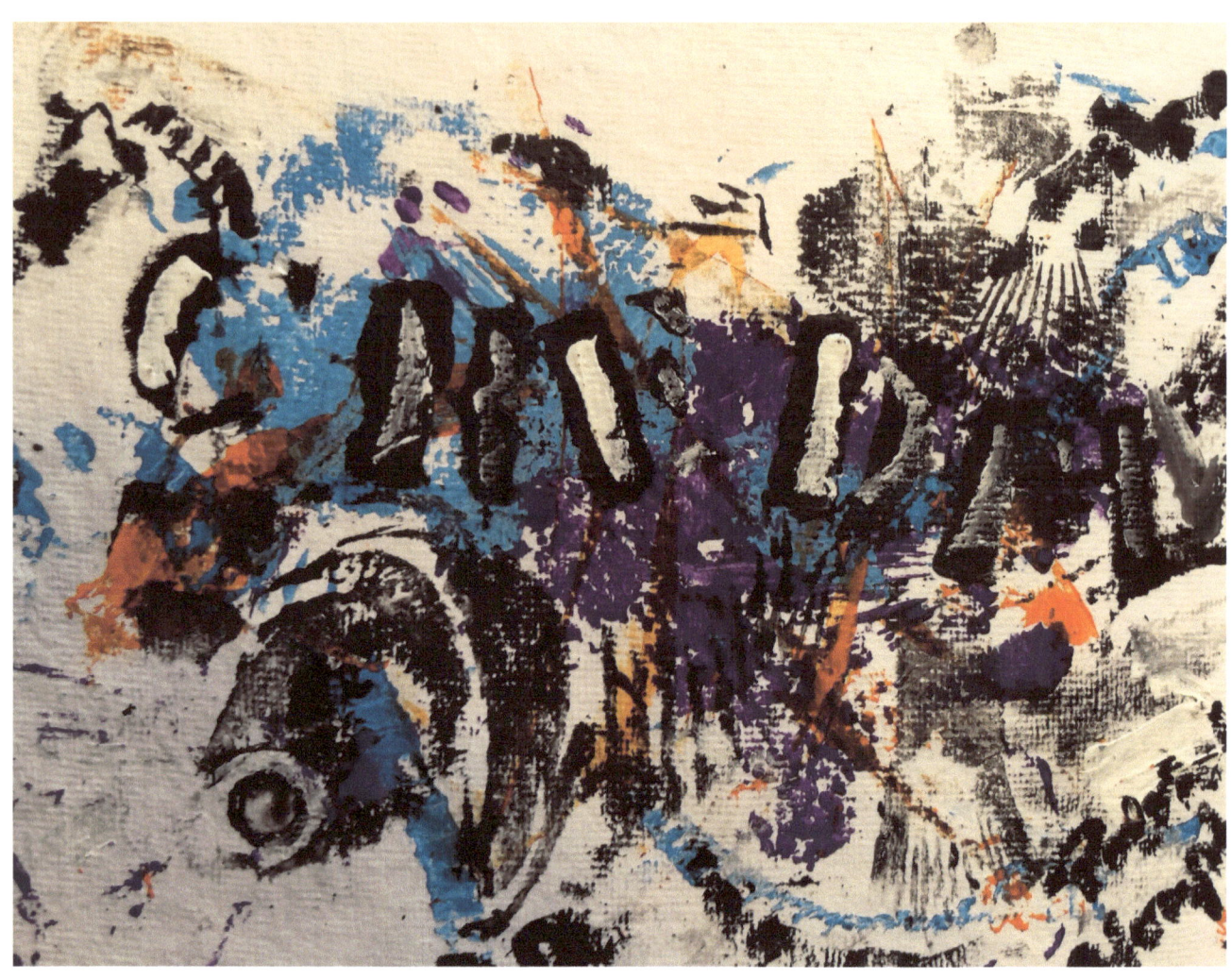

Figure 25 – you get CREDIT for looking at this piece !!??!! Just kidding . CREDIT is the dominate thing in this image. There are parts of fish , no complete fish there also is a seahorse in the upper left corner next to the letter C . So do you get CREDIT for finding the seahorse (maybe I will do a find and seek book next, my images lend well to this sentiment) . MAYBE ??!!!???

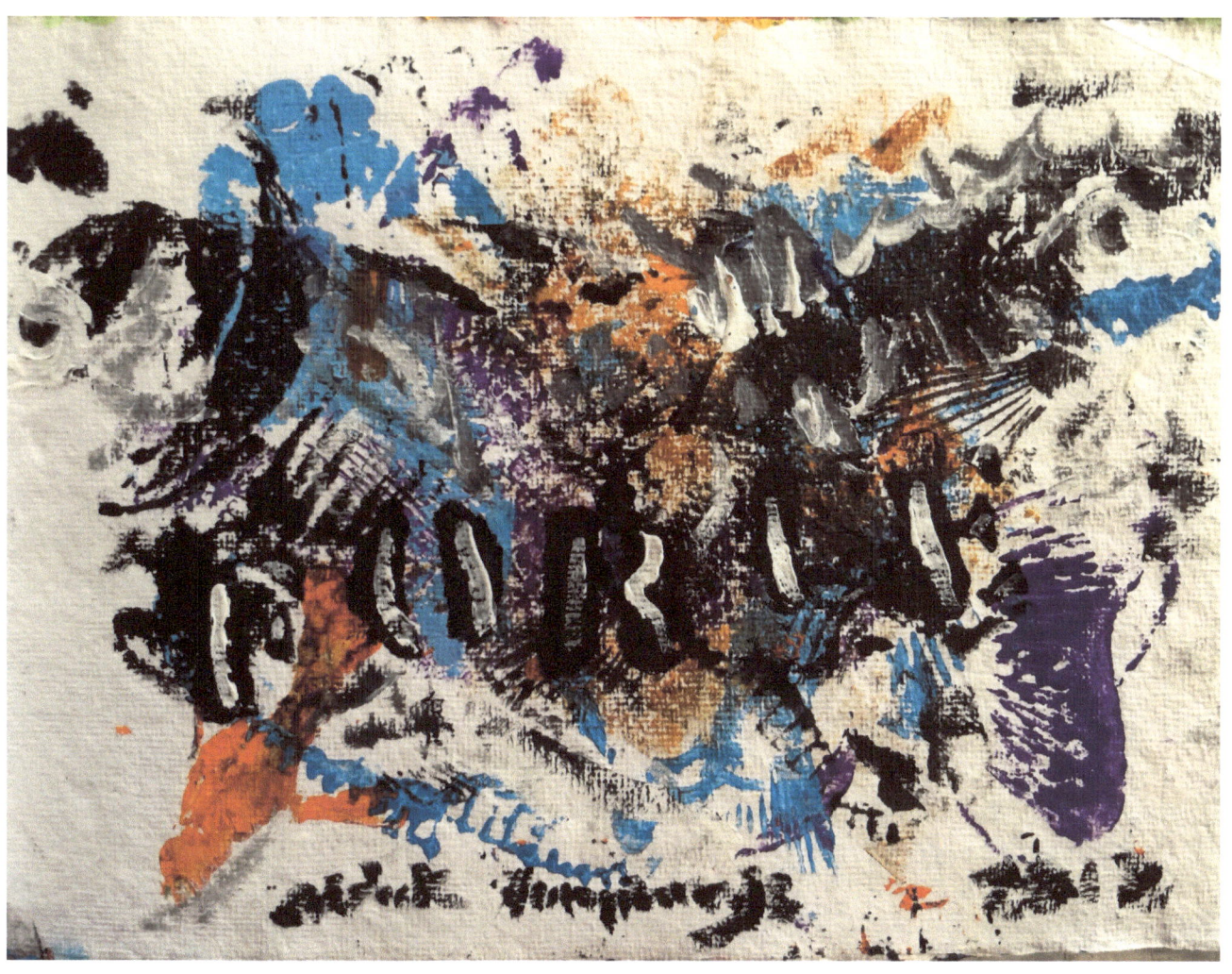

Figure 26- the dominate thing in this painting is the word PORIE . WHAT DOES THAT MEAN "PORIE" ?!!??!! IT IS CODE FOR SOMETHING I KNOW. WHAT IS THE CODE STAND FOR ??!!?? WHAT IS THE PRIMER ??!! ONLY I KNOW AND I WON'T TELL SO DON'T ASK. IT IS MY SECRET . MAYBE FOR A MILLION DOLLARS ???!!!

<u>APPENDIX</u>

SUPPLIES NEED TO CREATE GYOTABSTRACT

(1) Dead fish (from the sea, ocean or supermarket shelves) or fish molds purchased through Dick Blick Art Supplies or Acorn Naturalists Supplies. You can buy the fish molds from Dick Blick Art Supplies at www.dickblick.com and Acorn Naturalists Supplies at www.aconnaturalists.com .

(2) Printmaking supplies such as brayer, baren, ink, acrylic paint , and brushes from the above mentioned Dick Blick Art Supplies or Acorn Naturalists Supplies or from local art and craft stores such as JoAnn's Crafts, Michael's or Hobby Lobby.

BOOKS ABOUT GYOTAKU

(1) Fukuchi, Mitsuo, "Antarctic Fishes: Illustrated in the Gyotaku Method by Boshu Nagase, Rosenberg Publishing, 2006. THIS IS A GREAT BOOK, OVERSIZED BOOK WITH "REAL SIZED" GYOTAKU PRINTS OF THE FISH. HIGHLY RECOMMENDED!!!

(2) Hiyama , Yoshio, "Gyotaku: The Art and Technique of the Japanese Fish Print", University of Washington Press, 1964. VERY GOOD BOOK FOR TECHNIQUE.

(3) Olander, Doug, "Gyotaku Fish Impressions: The Art of Japanese Fish Printing", Frank Amato Publishing, 1994. VERY GOOD BOOK ! I HAD IN GRAD SCHOOL AT WESTERN MICHIGAN UNIVERSITY ! GREAT INTRODUCTION TO GYOTAKU !!!

That is about it for Gyotaku in books. There are a couple of ones in Japanese that I am unfamiliar with. Good luck hunting for other ones !!!
Also the internet is a good resource for information on Gyotaku.

MY OTHER BOOKS

(1) Balinese Beckoning, CreateSpace, 2013, ISBN: 978-1494804770.
(2) Broken Dreams, CreateSpace, 2013, ISBN: 978-1492734161.
(3) Divorce Diary, CreateSpace, 2013, ISBN: 978-148030257.

(4) drawn to believe, CreateSpace, 2013, ISBN: 978-1490568621.

(5) low key supermarket free verse, PublishAmerica, 2011, ISBN: 978-11462629787.

(6) Good Kitty with..., CreateSpace, 2013, ISBN: 978-149279333.

(7) It's just a scratch, CreateSpace, 2103, ISBN: 978-1484156728.

(8) flowers and sweets, CreateSpace, 2014, ISBN: 978-1495211843.

(9) Rock Hard Cupcake and Dead Fish, CreateSpace, 2013, ISBN: 978-1490433080.

(10)   Rock Hard Cupcake and Dead Fish, black and white version, CreateSpace, 2013, ISBN: 978-149792039.

(11)   Tainted Visions, CreateSpace, 2014, ISBN: 978-1495272189.

(12)   Visual Dissection, CreateSpace, 2013, ISBN: 978-1482797015.

(13)   Whatever book, CreateSpace, 2013, ISBN: 978-149790653.

(14)   Zombie Stick Man Blues, CreateSpace, 2013, ISBN: 978-1483961200.

(15)   Where it comes from, CreateSpace, 2013, ISBN: 978-1484098868.

(16)   Mayan Free Verse, CreateSpace, 2014, ISBN: 978-1494912543.

(17)   OSM : WL Condition, CreateSpace, 2013, ISBN: 978-1484192870.

(18)   Scratching for a reason to live, CreateSpace, ISBN: 978-1484875988.

(19)   no captions needed: toy paintings/drawings, CreateSpace, ISBN: 978-1484940204.

(20)   Wayang Kulit: a painter's interpretation, CreateSpace, ISBN: 978-1490320083.

(21)   1,2,3 kitties : a cat counting book, PublishAmerica, 2008, ISBN: 978-160610848.

(22)   48708, +/-, &/or: an artist's life, CreateSpace, 2014, ISBN: 978-1494854232.

THANKS FOR PURCHASING THIS BOOK!!!

I WANT TO DEDICATE THIS BOOK TO MY SON, CAMERON !!!
I LOVE YOU SO MUCH!!!!

www.ingramcontent.com/pod-product-compliance
Lightning Source LLC
Chambersburg PA
CBHW050911180526
45159CB00007B/2872